J   5434428
532   14.95
Pea
Peacock
Water

Water

Graham Peacock

Thomson Learning • New York

Books in the series:

ASTRONOMY • ELECTRICITY • FORCES
HEAT • LIGHT • MATERIALS
SOUND • WATER

First published in the
United States in 1994 by
Thomson Learning
115 Fifth Avenue
New York, NY 10003

First published in Great Britain in 1994 by
Wayland (Publishers) Ltd.

Library of Congress Cataloging-in-Publication Data
Peacock, Graham.
    Water / Graham Peacock.
        p.   cm. – (Science activities)
    Includes bibliographical references and index.
    ISBN: 1-56847-077-0
    1. Water – Juvenile literature. 2. Water –
Experiments – Juvenile literature. [1. Water –
Experiments. 2. Experiments.] I. Title. II. Series.
QC920.P43   1994
532'.0078 – dc20   93-49799

Printed in Italy

Acknowledgments
The publishers would like to thank the following for allowing
their pictures to be used in this book: Science Photo Library 27, 29;
Tony Stone Images 4, 7, 15. All commissioned photographs
are from the Wayland Picture Library (Zul Mukhida).
All artwork is by Tony de Saulles.

Contents

Words that appear in **bold** are explained in the glossary on page 30.

Water drops

Water is the most common substance on Earth. It covers about three-quarters of Earth's surface in the form of vast oceans and seas. Life itself is believed to have started in the seas many millions of years ago, and all living things contain water. Without water, Earth would be as lifeless as the moon. Water is the only substance that occurs naturally as a gas, a liquid, and a solid. Many materials can dissolve in water. Many drinks, such as soda and coffee, are no more than water in which a few ingredients have been dissolved. In this book there are many activities that will help you to understand more about water.

Three ways of making water drops

You will need:

- ◆ a straw ◆ a spoon
- ◆ a medicine dropper

Watch what happens when water drops land in a glass of water.

Put your straw in some water. Place your finger over the top of the straw and take it out of the water. Make a drop by taking away your finger slightly.

Use a medicine dropper to make different-sized drops.

Gently shake drops from the back of a spoon.

What happens to water on different surfaces?

You will need:

◆ shiny paper ◆ a dropper ◆ 3 leaves ◆ a candle or a wax crayon ◆ a feather
◆ writing paper ◆ assorted paper and pieces of plastic (optional) ◆ a pencil

1 Put a single drop of water on the shiny paper.

What shape is it?

2 Looking from the side, draw the drop.

3 Put a drop of water on the feather. Roll it back and forth.

4 Put a drop on the leaves.

Which leaves make the drops flat and which make them like a ball?

Make drops on other kinds of paper, such as a paper towel, and plastic.

Waterproofing

Rub one half of a piece of writing paper with a candle or wax crayon.

Put a drop of water on each half.

Explain what you see.

Did you know?

When the drop is fat and round, it is because the water is **repelled** by the surface.

Surfaces that **attract** water make the drops flat.

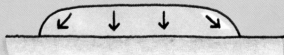

Water's skin

Can you see and feel water's skin?

You will need:

- a glass ◆ a sieve ◆ a plastic lid
- a rubber band ◆ a knife

1 Fill a clean glass to the brim with water.

2 Slowly add more water until you can see its surface just above the rim of the glass.

Skin pull

1 Cut a hole in a clean plastic lid.

2 Thread a rubber band through the hole and drop the lid onto the water.

3 Feel how hard you have to pull the rubber band to lift the lid slowly off the water's skin.

Water in holes

1 Gently place a dry sieve on some water. Why doesn't it sink right away?

2 Look at the sieve when you take it out. Why does the water still hang in the holes?

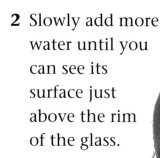

Which things can rest on the surface skin?

You will need:

- ◆ a bowl ◆ tissue paper ◆ a small paper clip
- ◆ a pin or needle ◆ a piece of aluminum foil

1 Pour water into the bowl.

2 Put a small piece of tissue paper on the surface of the water. Rest a pin on the tissue.

3 Watch what happens once the tissue paper sinks. (Be patient, as this may take a minute or two.)

Try resting other small objects, such as a paper clip or piece of aluminum foil, on the water's skin.

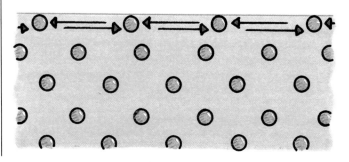

Surface tension

The skin of water is caused by **surface tension**. The **molecules** of water attract each other. Those at the surface attract each other most strongly, so they seem to form a skin.

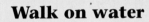

Walk on water

Some small animals, such as the water strider, can stand on the water's skin.

Soaking in

Which materials soak up water the fastest?

You will need:

- assorted pieces of paper and fabric
- a shallow tank or pan
- a thin piece of wood about 2 feet long ◆ drawing paper ◆ pen
- thumbtacks or tape

1 Cut the paper and fabric into equal-sized strips.

Predict which will soak up water the quickest.

2 Tack or tape your samples to the piece of wood.

3 Hang the wood over the tank, filled with water, so that the water touches the bottom of each strip.

4 Using a pen, mark how far the water has soaked up on each strip.

thin paper   felt   cloth   tissue

thick paper   sponge   cotton   crepe paper

In our test, tissue soaked up water the quickest.

Which colors spread out the farthest?

You will need:

- ♦ paper towel or blotting paper
- ♦ water-soluble felt-tip pens (not waterproof pens)
- ♦ a dropper

1 Using a black or brown pen, make a small mark on a paper towel.

2 Carefully drip three or four drops of water onto the ink mark.

3 Wait three to four minutes until the water has stopped spreading out.

Look at the colored rings that have spread around the ink mark.

Each color is made up of different **pigments**. Some travel farther through the paper than others. This process by which the different pigments are separated is called **chromatography**.

Find out:

- ● which color has the greatest number of pigments.

Capillary action

Tissues and newspapers are made of fibers. The fibers are like very fine tubes. They draw up water by **capillary action**.

Washing science

What does detergent do to water?

You will need:

♦ a piece of cardboard ♦ a dropper
♦ liquid detergent ♦ cloth ♦ cotton

1 Rub a little liquid **detergent** onto part of the cardboard.

2 Put one drop of water on the untreated cardboard. Put another drop on the part with detergent.

3 Compare the shapes of the two water drops. Which one wets the cardboard faster?

Detergents break down water's skin. This helps water to wet things.

Soapy tests

Do you think that clean water will drip through cloth more slowly than water that has detergent in it? Test your idea.

Will a piece of cotton sink faster in clean or soapy water? Plan a test to find out. (Each piece of cotton should be the same size.)

Why do we use laundry detergent?

You will need:

◆ small, identical pieces of white cloth ◆ jars with blank labels
◆ laundry soap ◆ safety bleach

1 Make the pieces of cloth equally dirty. (You can stain them all with things like grass, orange juice, or soil.)

2 Test different ways of cleaning the pieces of cloth.

● You could soak them in cold water.

● You could soak them in warm water (not too hot).

● You could rub each piece of cloth as it soaks.

How will you make all the tests fair?

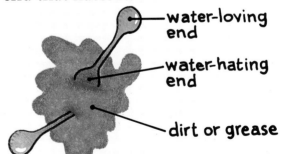

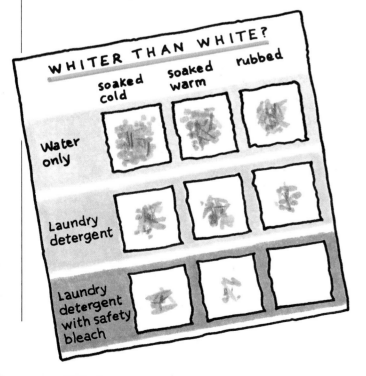

WHITER THAN WHITE?

	soaked cold	soaked warm	rubbed
Water only			
Laundry detergent			
Laundry detergent with safety bleach			

Did you know?

Detergent molecules have one end that loves water and one end that hates it.

- water-loving end
- water-hating end
- dirt or grease

The detergent molecules pull the grease off the cloth because one end is attracted to the water.

11

Dissolving

Which things dissolve in water?

You will need:

- small glasses or jars
- powders from the kitchen (for example, baking soda, sugar, salt, flour, instant coffee) ◆ clean spoons

1 Fill each glass with water. Add a teaspoon of one of the powders to each glass. (Use a different spoon for each powder.)

2 Stir the water. Leave it for a few minutes.

3 Does the powder **dissolve**?

How could you record your results?

Look carefully

Dissolves:

- you can see through the water

- nothing is left on the bottom of the glass

Does not dissolve:

- the water is cloudy

- powder is left on the bottom of the glass

Where does it go?

When a material dissolves, it is broken up into tiny particles that spread out through the water.

particles of the solid spread out

water particles

How can you make things dissolve more quickly?

You will need:

- glasses or jars ◆ sugar ◆ teaspoons
- salt ◆ a timer

Plan a test to see whether sugar dissolves faster in warm or cold water.

Find out:

- if stirring makes the sugar dissolve more quickly.

- if the amount of water affects how quickly the sugar dissolves.

Will more sugar dissolve if the water is warm?

1 Count the number of spoonfuls of sugar you can dissolve in a glass of cold water.

2 Count how many spoonfuls of sugar will dissolve in a glass of hot water.

3 Plan a test to see if salt behaves in the same way. What is your prediction?

Seawater

Most of the salt dissolved in seawater is common table salt (sodium chloride). Seawater contains several other kinds of salt as well.

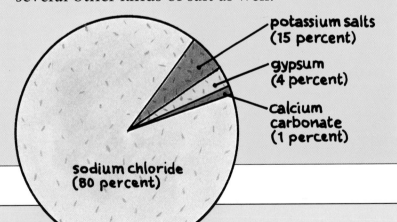

potassium salts (15 percent)

gypsum (4 percent)

calcium carbonate (1 percent)

sodium chloride (80 percent)

Did you know?

Cold water dissolves air better than warm water.

If you leave a glass of cold water in a warm place, bubbles appear on the inside of the glass. This is the air coming out of the **solution**.

Salt water

How can you grow salt crystals?

You will need:

♦ salt ♦ 3 dishes

1 Make a very strong solution of salt water.

2 Pour the salt water into the dishes.

● Let one solution **evaporate** in a warm room.

● Let one evaporate over a radiator or in the sunshine.

● Let one evaporate slowly in a cool place.

3 Are there any differences in the **crystals** that form?

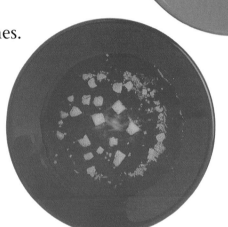

You can get dissolved solids back by letting the water evaporate.

More crystals

Warning! Do not drink these solutions or get them in your eyes. Some are poisonous!

1 Ask an adult to buy some alum, epsom salts, copper sulfate, or similar powdery substances from a pharmacy.

2 Use these powders to make three very strong solutions.

3 Allow the water to evaporate slowly.

4 Draw pictures of the crystals left over.

Compare salt water and fresh water

Will salt water harm plants?

You will need to grow two pots of cress plants or grass to find out.

Does salt water freeze as quickly as fresh water?

How will you check that the test is fair?

Does salt water weigh the same as fresh?

Plan your test carefully. Make sure your measurements are accurate.

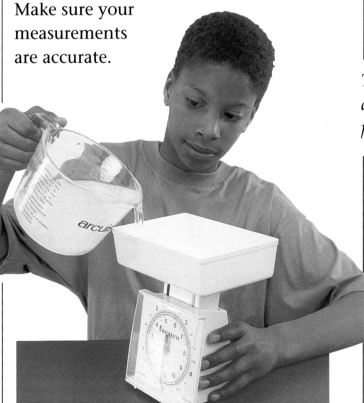

The water in the Dead Sea is much saltier and denser than normal seawater, so people find it easier to float.

Did you know?

The water level of the Dead Sea in Israel is below the level of other seas. Rivers only flow into the Dead Sea; no rivers flow out. Therefore, water can only escape by evaporation. This means that Dead Sea water is much saltier than normal seawater.

Cleaning dirty water

Which is the best design for a water filter?

You will need:

- 3 plastic bottles
- cotton ◆ sand
- small stones
- gravel ◆ paper
- dirty water
- 3 glasses or jars

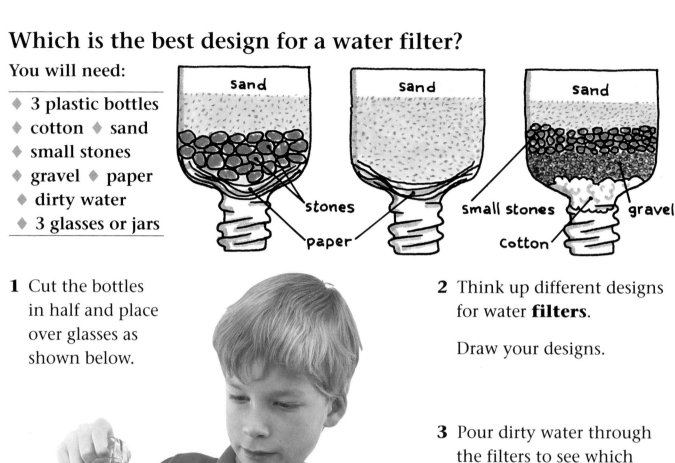

sand · sand · sand

stones

paper

small stones · gravel

cotton

1 Cut the bottles in half and place over glasses as shown below.

2 Think up different designs for water **filters**.

Draw your designs.

3 Pour dirty water through the filters to see which works best.

1 2 3

Which paper makes the best water filter?

You will need:

- different types of paper ◆ a plate
- a pencil ◆ scissors ◆ a funnel

1 Using the plate, draw a circle on each piece of paper and cut it out.

2 Fold the paper circle in half. Then fold it into quarters.

3 Open the quarters out into a cone shape. Put it into the funnel.

4 Which paper cone is the best filter?

Did you know?
Water from all the major rivers in the United States is used, poured down drains, then filtered and reused many times between its source and the sea.

Water works

water is held in tanks to let some mud settle

water is sifted to remove some more solid pieces

water is filtered through sand and gravel

fine sand

coarse gravel

chlorine is added to kill germs

clean drinking water

17

Water pressure

Where does water press the hardest?

You will need:

◆ **a plastic bottle** ◆ **tape** ◆ **a knife**

1 Carefully make three holes at different heights above each other in the side of the plastic bottle.

2 Put a piece of tape over all three holes.

3 Fill the bottle with water.

4 Stand the bottle with the holes pointing toward a sink or a bowl. Pull off the tape.

Why do you think that the bottom jet of water travels the farthest?

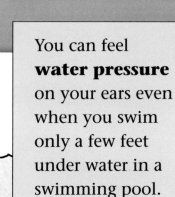

You can feel **water pressure** on your ears even when you swim only a few feet under water in a swimming pool.

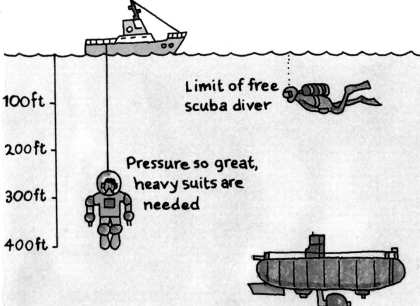

100ft

200ft

300ft

400ft

Limit of free scuba diver

Pressure so great, heavy suits are needed

Really deep

In 1960, the U.S. **bathyscaphe** *Trieste* descended more than 35,000 feet into the Mariana Trench in the Pacific Ocean.

How do fountains work?

You will need:

- a plastic bottle
- 2 feet of plastic tubing
- modeling clay ◆ knife

1 Make a single hole near the bottom of the bottle. The hole must be a little smaller around than the plastic tubing.

2 Push the tubing a little way into the hole. Seal around it with the clay.

3 Fill the bottle with water.

4 Raise and lower the end of the tube.

What happens to the height of the fountain?

Find out:

- what happens when you replace the bottle top.

Garden fountains

Most modern fountains use electric pumps.

Old fountains use water pressure from lakes high above the garden.

lake in hills above the garden

underground pipe leading to fountain

garden fountain

Waterwheels

Make your own waterwheels

You will need:

♦ an empty thread spool ♦ modeling clay ♦ a pencil ♦ a pitcher

1 Put modeling clay around the spool.

2 Make buckets in the clay.

3 Put a pencil through the spool. Run water slowly onto the buckets from a pitcher or a faucet.

Find out:

● if more buckets make the wheel turn faster.

● if larger buckets help.

● what happens when you hold the wheel closer to the faucet or pitcher.

trough

Overshot wheel

Overshot wheels are much more efficient than undershot wheels

Undershot wheel

Paddle steamers

Warning! Be careful with the knife!

You will need:

- ♦ a large cork ♦ a plastic lid
- ♦ scissors ♦ a sharp knife
- ♦ 2 pins

1 Ask an adult to use the knife. Carefully cut four slits into the cork.

2 From the plastic lid, cut four blades the same length as the cork.

3 Push the blades into the slits in the cork. Push the pins into each end of the cork.

4 Hold the wheel by the pins under slowly running water.

Paddle steamers used waterwheels instead of propellers to move them through the water.

True or false?

1 Scuba divers can dive down to 600 feet.
2 Duck feathers attract water.
3 Water striders stand on the water's skin.
4 A chromatogram is a measure of weight, like a kilogram.
5 Detergents pull grease off clothes.
6 Seawater contains at least four types of dissolved salt.
7 Water can dissolve air.
8 The Dead Sea is very salty.
9 Drinking water is filtered through sand.
10 Blotting paper repels water.   Answers on page 32.

Floating

Which things float in water?

You will need:

- a bowl or tank of water
- pieces of plastic ♦ a rubber band
- a ball ♦ small metal objects

Put the objects in the water to see which ones will float.

Has it sunk?

Unless an object is resting on the bottom of the tank, it is **floating.**

Why do things float? Is it the air in them?

You will need:

- a sponge
- a candle
- an eraser
- a piece of plastic
- a plastic ball
- an ice cube

1 Squeeze all the air out of the sponge. Put it in the water.

Does it still float?

2 Check that the other objects have no air in them.

Do they float?

Water pushes back

You will need:

◆ **a ball or balloon** ◆ **a tank of water**

Push a balloon under water. Can you feel the water pushing back as more of the balloon is forced under water?

Why do things float?

Objects that weigh less than the same volume of water float.

One gallon of ice weighs less than one gallon of water.

You will need:

◆ **a stone**
◆ **rubber bands**
◆ **a tank of water**

1 Hang a clean stone from some rubber bands.

2 Predict what will happen to the pull on the rubber bands when you hang the stone in water.

Will the weight of the stone seem heavier, lighter, or the same?

Give reasons for your prediction.

Boats and submarines

Why do boats float?

You will need:

♦ modeling clay ♦ marbles or other small objects ♦ a measuring cup

1 Find out if a ball of clay floats.

2 What happens if you make the clay ball into a saucer shape?

Does the saucer shape float like a boat?

It takes the place of water

1 Half fill a measuring cup with water.

2 Put the ball of clay into the jug.

How high does the water rise?

3 Make a boat shape from the clay ball.

How high does the water rise now?

Does the ball or the boat shape push more water out of the way?

Find out:
● what happens to the level of the water in the cup when you add weights to the boat shape.

marbles

Make a toy diver

You will need:

◆ a clear plastic bottle with cap ◆ a medicine dropper
◆ a pitcher of water ◆ paper clips

1 Hang paper clips on the dropper so that it just floats in the pitcher of water.

2 Put the dropper into the bottle of water. Put the cap on the bottle.

3 Gently squeeze the bottle. The diver should sink.

4 Stop squeezing. The diver should rise.

5 Can you make the diver hover?

How it works

When you squeeze the bottle, the air in the dropper is squashed and is replaced by water. This makes the dropper heavier, so it sinks.

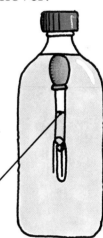

watch the water level

Swim bladders

Bony fish have air-filled swim bladders. They use the swim bladders to change their weight so that they can swim at different depths.

swim bladder

Sharks do not have swim bladders. Some sharks would sink if they didn't swim constantly.

We need water

How much water do living things contain?

You will need:

- pieces of fresh bread ◆ a carrot
- slices of apple ◆ a baking tray
- a warm oven (below 350°F)
- kitchen scales

1 Weigh each piece of food.

2 Put the food on the baking tray. Put the tray into the oven. (If it is sunny, you could dry the food out in the sunshine instead.)

3 When the food has dried, take the tray out of the oven. Weigh the food again to see which piece contained the most water.

Dried food

1 Weigh some dried kidney beans or lima beans.

2 Soak them for two hours in water.

3 See if you can find out how much water the beans have soaked up.

Warning! Do not eat red kidney beans unless they are cooked. They are poisonous when they are uncooked.

Why do people sweat?

You will need:

- ◆ **dampened tissue paper**
- ◆ **a small fan**

1 Wipe the tissue paper on the back of your hand.

2 Let the breeze from the fan blow over the dampened skin.

3 What does it feel like? Does the breeze feel different on dry skin?

Water use

Figure out how much water you use every day. Every time you flush the toilet, 10 quarts of water go down the drain.

Did you know?

In the United States, people use some 400 billion gallons of water each day.

Keeping cool in fur

Furry animals cannot **sweat**.

Dogs lose heat by evaporating water from their tongues.

The white of this heat image shows where the squash player is hottest and the blue where he is most cool.

Plants need water

How much water do cress seeds need?

You will need:

- cress or other fast-growing seeds
- plant soil ◆ a teaspoon
- 4 small flowerpots ◆ labels

1 Put soil into each flowerpot and plant the seeds.

2 Label each pot with the number of teaspoons of water you are going to give the seeds in that pot.

3 Put the pots in a sunny place. After watering them for two weeks, decide which seeds have grown the best.

How much water does a large plant use?

You will need:

- a dandelion or daisy
- a bottle with a wide neck
- modeling clay

1 Wash the flower's roots.

2 Fill the bottle with water. Put the flower up to the top of its roots into the water and carefully seal around the bottle top with clay.

3 Keep the bottle in a bright place. How much water does the flower take out of the bottle in one week?

Find out:

- what happens if you put a clear plastic bag over the plant.

- if a large plant uses more water than a small one.

- if the plant uses more water in the sun than in the shade.

Which part of a plant draws up water?

You will need:

- ◆ a piece of celery with its leaves
- ◆ a glass of water dyed red
- ◆ a glass of water dyed blue

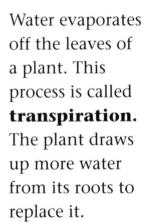

1 Split the stem of the celery in two for half of its length. Put one half of the stem in the red water and the other in the blue water.

2 Prop the celery safely against a wall.

3 After two days, cut through the two halves of the stem to see the plant's water tubes. What happens to the celery leaves when the stems are in the colored water?

White flowers

Try the same experiment with a white flower. Split the stem and make it two-colored.

Water evaporates off the leaves of a plant. This process is called **transpiration.** The plant draws up more water from its roots to replace it.

Plants that need little water

Lichens grow on bare rock. The only time they take in water is when it rains.

◄ *Cacti in the Arizona desert store water in their stems. Cacti can last for many years before their water supplies run out.*

Glossary

Attract To pull toward itself – for example, blotting paper attracts water.

Bathyscaphe A deep-sea diving craft that can dive to great depths.

Capillary action In plants, this is the movement of water into the tiny tubes of a plant's stem.

Chromatography A way of separating pigments by passing water through them, using an absorbent material.

Crystals Geometrically shaped groups of particles found in a solid. Salt crystals, for example, are shaped like cubes.

Detergent A chemical that breaks down the surface tension of water.

Dissolve For a solid to mix with a liquid so that its particles become spread out among those of the liquid.

Evaporate To change from a liquid into a gas.

Filters Devices that can separate solids from liquids or gases when they are mixed together.

Floating Hovering in water, or resting on the water's surface.

Lichens Plants that are a combination of a fungus and an alga.

Molecules Tiny particles that make up a material. Water molecules are made up of hydrogen and oxygen.

Pigments The substances that give an object its color (by reflecting or absorbing light).

Repelled Pushed away. Water molecules are repelled by some materials; for example, wax and grease.

Solution A mixture made up of particles of a solid that are evenly spread out among those of a liquid.

Surface tension The "skin" on water, caused by the pull between the molecules at the water's surface.

Sweat Salty water that comes out of special pores onto the surface of the skin. Sweat cools you as it evaporates.

Transpiration The way in which water evaporates from plant leaves, mainly through tiny holes on the underside of the leaves.

Water pressure The force of water pressing on something. As an object goes deeper in water, the water pressure on it increases.

Water-soluble Able to dissolve in water.

Books to read

Baines, John. *Water*. Resources. New York: Thomson Learning, 1993.

Davies, Kay and Oldfield, Wendy. *Floating and Sinking*. Starting Science. Austin: Raintree Steck-Vaughn, 1991.

Devonshire, Hilary. *Water*. Science Through Art. New York: Franklin Watts, 1992.

Richards, Roy. *101 Science Tricks: Fun Experiments with Everyday Materials*. New York: Sterling Publishing Co., 1991.

Twist, Clint. *Rain to Dams: Projects with Water*. Hands On Science. New York: Gloucester Press, 1990.

Ward, Alan. *Experimenting with Surface Tension and Bubbles*. Experimenting With. New York: Chelsea House, 1991.

Chapter notes

Pages 4–5 Making single drops takes dexterity and practice. The waxed side of the paper will repel the water, causing the drop to be rounded.

Pages 6–7 It is important that the glass and bowl are both very clean. The bonds between water molecules behave like springs and the attraction increases the farther apart they are. The molecules at the water's surface are slightly farther apart than the rest, and this gives water its characteristic skin.

Pages 8–9 The pigments in chromatography must be soluble in water. The distance traveled by the pigments depends on their degree of solubility and their attraction to the paper.

Capillary action is caused by the attraction of the water molecules to the sides of the tiny tubes (capillaries) formed by coarse paper such as tissue paper or newspaper. Shiny paper used for magazines are filled with china clay. This blocks the tubes, resulting in very little capillary action.

Pages 10–11 Detergents help to wet things more rapidly. They break down the surface tension of water, remove grease, and keep dirt suspended in the water. Enzymes help to break down proteins and loosen dirt. Detergents are added to things such as insecticides and weed killers to help them work more rapidly and effectively.

Pages 12–13 When a solid is added to a liquid, the solid (solute) particles spread out evenly in the liquid (solvent). A solid that has not dissolved can be suspended, as when mud and water are mixed, or it can form a colloid. Milk is a colloid of fat and water.

Pages 14–15 Make sure that you do not drink any water that has been used in any experiment.

To make salty water evaporate slowly, you can put it in a freezer as it is unlikely to freeze. Seawater stays liquid well below the freezing point of pure water. Mono Lake in California is a natural soda lake, but as water is being diverted from entering the lake, the remaining water is becoming extremely salty.

Pages 16–17 Make your own water filter from your designs. The finer the materials used, the more effective the filter, but the flow rate is faster with coarser materials.

Pages 18–19 Water pressure does not just press down. Like air pressure, it operates at all angles. Water supply to houses often comes from tanks standing on towers. Notice that in the fountain activity, the level of the water in the tube is at the same height as the level in the bottle.

Pages 20–21 Large waterwheels were one of the first sources of power used in industry. The important factor is the amount by which the water drops (this is called the head of water). Modern water turbines are more like propellers than waterwheels.

Pages 22–23 Objects float if their density is less than that of water. Water has a density of 1 gram (g) per cubic centimeter. If an object, such as a sponge, contains air, this may give it a total density of less than 1 g per cubic centimeter. When water freezes, it expands. This means that ice has a lower density than liquid water.

Pages 24–25 Boats float because their total density is less than 1 g per cubic centimeter. Look at the volume of water that a boat shape displaces. The boat shape displaces a greater volume of water than the same amount of clay in a ball shape.

When you squeeze the plastic bottle, look carefully at the level of water in the glass tube of the dropper. It rises because the air in the dropper bulb can be squashed, but the water is incompressible.

Page 26–27 We get much of the water we need from the food we eat. Dried food absorbs large quantities of water. When drying the pieces of food, it is important to keep them in the air. Do not cover them, or the food may turn moldy before it dries.

A moving breeze cools us because it speeds the evaporation of water from our skin. The moving air need not be cool to have this effect. If you measure the temperature of air from a cooling fan, you will see that it is the same temperature as the still air.

Pages 28–29 In the first activity on this page, it is important to control all the other variables in the experiment. The variable you are changing, the amount of water, is the independent variable. Always remember what you are changing and what you are keeping the same.

Index

Answers to questions on page 21:
1 false, 2 false, 3 true, 4 false, 5 true, 6 true, 7 true 8 true, 9 true, 10 false